Unmirrored
FACES,
Mirrored
HEARTS

OUR FAMILY'S HOPE-FILLED MULTICULTURAL ADOPTION
OF AN OLDER CHILD

Sophia Blake

WESTBOW
PRESS®
A DIVISION OF THOMAS NELSON
& ZONDERVAN

WestBow Press books may be ordered through booksellers or by contacting:

WestBow Press
A Division of Thomas Nelson & Zondervan
1663 Liberty Drive
Bloomington, IN 47403
www.westbowpress.com
1 (866) 928-1240

ISBN: 978-1-5127-0876-9 (sc)
ISBN: 978-1-5127-0875-2 (e)

Library of Congress Control Number: 2015913420

Print information available on the last page.

WestBow Press rev. date: 09/01/2015

Contents

Prologue

I had walked into an adoption agency in May 2008 to meet a girl who could very well become our daughter. I expected to gaze into the tiny, fragile face of a young girl who looked like a mix of my husband and me. Instead, I encountered a tall girl with gorgeous cocoa skin. She was a five-year-old who looked more like eight and seemed big enough to be able to hold me in her lap. She picked up all she possessed, which was contained in a large, old Tupperware tub. She looked me straight in the eye, with a tear in hers, and said, "Okay, I'm ready."

Chapter 1

Something Was Missing

In 1998, my husband, Aiden, and I had never discussed adopting a child. We already had two gorgeous biological boys whose births had involved two very difficult, painful labors and deliveries. My physicians had told me that the mother must be at least *four centimeters* dilated for a doctor to administer an epidural to manage the pain and a mightily impressive *ten centimeters* for the delivery to be accomplished. As was the case in my first son's birth, I stayed at two centimeters for approximately fourteen hours before rapidly progressing to the ten centimeters that one must be at to push a child into the world.

They say you forget the pain when you finally hold your child for the first time. Fortunately for me, the first time I gave birth, I did forget. Perhaps when I pushed out my first son I also pushed my memory of the difficulties, because I became pregnant again about two years later. Then I definitely remembered the pain I had experienced, especially after the unfortunate tearing of some delicate tissue in that second delivery.

Our first son came out looking almost identical to my husband. The aquamarine eyes and pale skin on my sweet baby were beautiful but left me wondering whether **I** had actually given birth to this child. When I became pregnant with our second son, I was certain he would look more like me, since brown eyes and brown hair are usually dominant traits. I had learned this in my biology courses in college, and after all, I carried him almost nine months! Didn't

I have the right to have one child look even remotely like me? The answer was a resounding *no,* as I saw my second green-eyed little boy coming into the world with a sprinkle of blond hair and holding on to the umbilical cord for dear life.

As my babies grew into toddlers and threw the occasional tantrum, an inordinate amount of bystanders gawked and stared confusedly as this mocha-skinned, brown-eyed, red-faced mommy hurriedly carried a screaming little boy out of a store. Too many people asked, "Is he *yours*?" The comments grew tiresome as I remembered the heartburn and sleepless nights and excruciating deliveries. Being mistaken for the nanny was starting to get irritating as well! I never would have guessed that these experiences with total strangers were part of God's preparation. Certainly I loved our boys and was content to be a mother of two. But for some reason, I had the nagging feeling that something was missing.++

I began gushing too often at babies, especially little girls. I loved their cute, flouncy dresses. I loved their precious little bloomers with ruffles that resembled five-layer wedding cakes. They were Hispanic, Caucasian, African-American, Asian—but all that mattered to me was that they were girls. I knew I was not willing to go through pregnancy and labor again, even as much as I realized what a miracle and blessing it is to give birth biologically.

My boys were growing. They were around seven and four years old and were on lizard quests at the time. Almost daily, the boys attached strings to lizards and paraded them proudly around the yard! Also, the boys enjoyed letting the little reptiles clamp onto their ears to look like earrings to *scare* Mom. Cars, turtles, video games, and mud seemed to be the standard at our house. But I longed to sit down to a tea party, choose outfits for Barbie, or visit a store without hearing "Can we go play video games now?"

Everywhere I went, the most beautiful clothes on display were for little girls. Pink blankets, pink bunnies, and even pink little cowgirl boots seemed to fill every store window. Feeling particularly inspired one afternoon as we drove over to Grandma's house, I decided to ask my sons if they wanted a little sister. I could have guessed their responses. Have you ever heard the sound of little boys pretending to gag?

Chapter 2

Journey Begins

In 2001, Aiden and I had touched on the idea of adoption. But we had never delved deeply into the subject, as he was busy doing his best at work to make a difference and get ahead. We had both recently become Christians as well. We were attending a nondenominational church in Texas. A mission trip to Saltillo, Mexico, was coming up; it involved getting an orphanage cleaned and stocked for some children who were to be sheltered there. Our very dear friends, the Williamses, planned to make the trip. After some consideration, we decided to go along. When I had first heard the trip announcement, my heart leaped. I didn't understand why it seemed like such a big deal, but I felt drawn to that orphanage; I needed to get to the bottom of my curiosity. I thought that if I saw for myself the conditions in which these children were living, I would know whether I wanted to continue down this road of adoption.

Upon traveling to Mexico, we arrived at the orphanage fairly early in the day. It had been kept in good condition. We proceeded to clean, assemble, and make up beds most of the day. We saw a few children walking alone in the streets, looking unkempt and slightly malnourished, but we did not get to interact with them much at the time. Even so, I had never obtained so much satisfaction in cleaning up and generally preparing a place to call home as I did that day.

The next morning, we departed from Saltillo. I wondered whose bed I had prepared, who would eat at the table I had cleaned, and who would use the supplies I had arranged. I knew those questions would not let my mind rest.

For months after we returned to the United States, I wrestled with the idea of caring for a child who was not biologically ours. Was this desire going to be quieted with time?

Not too long after the trip, I had an opportunity to help write and direct a Christmas play at our hometown church. Its theme was instilling character. We presented our play over the course of a week for twenty to thirty thousand kids from nearby towns. At the end of each performance, it was my duty to get up with my dearest friend, Kay, and reiterate the moral of the story. I thought I would die of a lack of oxygen as I stood up after the first performance. I was unable to breathe as I stared out at the 1,500 adults and children. I absolutely detested speaking in front of a crowd. You could say I had a phobia. But I made it through my part of the brief speech. At the end of each performance, as the play's closing song played over the speakers and these children stood and clapped their little hands with joy at the music and colorful characters on stage, I knew in my heart that my near asphyxiation was worth it!

I rested a few months before moving on to my next endeavor, which involved a cause that was dear to my heart. I volunteered for a nonprofit organization that was founded seven years earlier by another friend Maggie, whom I had assisted in writing a few scenes in the Christmas play.

This organization raised money to serve local abused and neglected children with blankets, clothes, stuffed animals, and even snacks when the children were removed from their homes to be placed in foster care. Usually, the children were taken swiftly for safety reasons and were unable to bring along any belongings. This organization also founded a nationally known awareness campaign that called upon churches to come together on the last Sunday in April to pray for an end to child abuse. Because of the sexual abuse I had suffered as a young child at the hand of distant relatives, I felt strongly about this cause—and others related to helping combat any abuse of a child.

While I am sharing these stages in my life that God took me through, it is not to gain sympathy or boast. These are not prerequisites for adoption; I don't wish to make you think I'm a saintly person. My family and friends know better. I share this with you because of its relevance to my personality and character. I believe God had to hold my hand and take me through these processes to bring me to the point of believing I could adopt and love a child not born of my womb. If you're reading this book and you've felt those flutters in your spirit, or your heart starts to beat a little faster when anyone mentions the word adoption. That is not a coincidence.

Chapter 3

Are We Adoptive Parent Material?

The early years of the new millennium continued to pass. By 2004, I knew that I wanted to do more for children. I was drawn to the idea of adoption once again. At that time, I knew one person in my life who was adopted: my younger cousin Angelica on my father's side.

Angelica had come to be a member of our large extended family at the age of two back in 1986. She was adopted by my Uncle Brian and Aunt Carrie. Carrie was more like an older sister to me; I admired and loved her dearly.

As Angelica was a young woman in 2004, I felt nosy asking her any questions on how she felt about being adopted. I thought it would evoke sadness or even resentment or she would think I was prying. Because of the fourteen-year age difference, we weren't as close as I would have liked to be. So, unfortunately, I didn't approach her for a child's perspective at that time.

I was unconvinced that Aiden and I were cut out to be adoptive parents—he and I had many differences. Our marriage, like so many others, had experienced its ups and downs. Many of them had to do with how completely opposite we were in our personalities and upbringings. To begin with, Aiden is Caucasian (his ancestors hailing from England) along with a tiny bit of Native American. I have a mix of Mexican, Spanish, and Slavic blood running through my veins.

As we grew up in the '70s and '80s, neither of our childhoods resembled *Leave It to Beaver*. But my husband's upbringing in the Church of Christ as a PK (preacher's kid) was quite opposite in some respects to my Pentecostal childhood. Of course, as we *both* were stubborn (and unsure of how we wanted to raise our own family), we had chosen to be married in a Presbyterian church in 1991.

After a brief honeymoon, we had started our marriage, living in eastern Texas.

I grew more and more concerned about our adoptive parenting skills as I recalled on several occasions our personal histories. Each of us had moved out of our parents' homes at young ages (Aiden at seventeen and I at nineteen). We had met at the ages of twenty and twenty-one and were married when I had just turned twenty-two. Aiden had put himself through school, and when we were married, I got a husband along with just over seventy-five thousand dollars of school loan debt.

We had spent most of the first ten years of our marriage trying to pay off this huge debt; with the births of our sons and our first mortgage, this task seemed especially daunting. We mulled over the fact that we had done okay so far raising two children. But what would happen if we added a third child who was not ours biologically? If you make a few mistakes with your biological children, you forgive yourself fairly easily. But in considering adoption, you start agonizing about making mistakes involving a child who would be entrusted to you by caseworkers, government officials, and attorneys. You start to get a little nervous. I would learn years later that this was all completely normal.

Chapter 4

Twenty-Four-Hour Daughter

It had been months since I had spoken to anyone about adoption. A few relatives and close friends had heard of our longings. But as life continued to be so busy for our household, we thought it might not be the right time to move forward regarding adoption.

One cool, fall afternoon as I started the nightly dinner preparation, my telephone rang. I answered as I chopped an onion for our stew. It was a good friend who I had met at the boys' elementary school. She said she had just received a call from a cousin who had befriended a young woman who had just given birth, a week prior, to a baby girl at a city hospital in eastern Texas. My heart began to beat faster as I guessed pretty quickly why my friend was giving me this information. This young mother reportedly had abandoned her baby at the hospital and had asked my friend's cousin to put the child up for adoption. The baby was currently living in another relative's home. As the woman who was the temporary caregiver was in no position to care for an infant, she needed someone to come get the baby immediately. I hung up the phone and called my husband at work.

At this point in our lives, we had no formal training or certificates from any adoption or foster care agencies. Our first priority, with our hearts not our heads leading the charge, was taking action to pick up that baby and bring her home. Aiden, through a work contact, obtained the name of a law firm where we could figure out all the legal proceedings for our new baby. This lawyer was generous enough to agree to see us *pro bono* or free of charge for one hour, as his usual rate of five hundred dollars was a bit steep for us then.

As we drove up to see the baby, my palms and forehead broke out into a sweat. We located the small but neatly kept clapboard house in a very modest part of town. A lady was waiting for us at the door with a tiny bundle wrapped in a yellow blanket. I peered into a red, scrunched-up little face. The baby's head had some of the blackest hair I had ever seen.

"Hi!" said the woman, who was the current caregiver. "I'm so glad you came. I've been calling in to my job for time off, and my son has also missed work in trying to care for the baby."

The biological mother, looking worn out and embarrassed, was also there; we had asked that she be present when we claimed our new daughter. We questioned the mother several times about her intentions for her baby. She reassured us that this was her wish. I inquired as to the whereabouts of the biological father. She looked away briefly before telling us that the likely father was incarcerated but she was not sure he was the one. There was another possible father, but neither of the men were interested in making any legal claims to their daughter.

We chatted briefly and informed them of our appointment the next morning at the lawyer's office. We said we would contact the biological mother when all the paperwork was done. You have to understand how utterly ignorant we were about all the legal premises and procedures. We figured that as long as legal documents were drawn up and everyone signed on the dotted line, the baby girl was ours. Adoption classes and background checks were not even remotely a thought in our heads.

Our baby was accompanied by a blanket, some diapers, two bottles, and a car seat. We carefully placed her in the car and buckled her in.

We promptly headed out for a Target store to buy a few little things to get us through the night. Aiden wanted to visit a consultant of his to discuss some work issues, so I dropped him off first.

At the store, as soon as I had secured the baby snugly in the shopping cart, a familiar aroma unpleasantly filled my nose. The cleaning up of a poo diaper,

I soon found out, was one of the unforeseen differences between a boy and a girl. Way more places for the poo to hide!

It had been a few years since I had handled an infant (my youngest son, Daniel, was six years old at this time). I got the baby cleaned up and situated in her seat. Off to the baby aisles we went. She was content to look at me as best she could. She occasionally made soft mewling noises. I was deeply engrossed in determining what kind of blanket material felt the softest when a fellow shopper stopped next to me.

"Oh, what a pretty baby!" the woman said. "She looks just like you!" The woman cooed at the infant. "What's her name?" she asked gently.

"Um, her name?" I replied, flushing instantly. "Oh, oh it's Si … Isabelle … Isabella … Bella for short." I also said, "Her middle name is Sophia." I hoped it did not sound like an afterthought. I could not believe I had not thought of a name.

"Well, she's precious," the woman said as she carted away.

"Th-thank you!" I replied, smiling, with relief showing on my face.

As I headed to the checkout with a *very* full cart and a hungry baby, I felt elated and overwhelmed at the same time. After I paid the hefty sum for all the baby products, we headed out the door and off to pick up Daddy from the consultant's office.

Aiden and I had called my mother-in-law earlier that morning with the news. Now, she joyfully awaited us with dinner and a place to stay that night. "Bella" went to sleep around 10:30 or 11:00 p.m. and proceeded to wake up every three to four hours for a feeding. My younger son had been an every-two-hours-feeding baby for almost four months, so I was accustomed to the sleep pattern. I rocked and sang to our new baby throughout the night; each time, she peacefully returned to sleep.

We were up at about seven o'clock the next day, as we had made a nine o'clock appointment for that morning and wanted to arrive early to the lawyer's office. Once there, we waited anxiously and watched as the minutes ticked by, past 9:00 a.m., to 9:10, then 9:25. Finally, the door opened and we were greeted by a tall, lanky fellow in his mid-forties to early fifties.

We chatted briefly about how we had come to think about adopting. Then we told him how we had found our new daughter. I noticed him looking nervously at both of us and then down at Bella in her carrier. He stopped Aiden in mid-sentence and pointed at Bella.

"Please tell me this is not the baby you're adopting," he said sternly. Aiden and I looked at each other, dumbfounded.

"Well … yes," we replied.

"I hate to tell you this," the lawyer said, "but you've already done everything wrong." I began to feel my heart hammering in my chest.

"First of all," he exclaimed, "the biological mother needed to relinquish her rights in writing and the baby had to be handed over to social services legally since you are not related to her in any way."

Then he asked, "Where is the biological father?"

"We know one possibility is in jail; the other is not in the picture," I said reservedly.

"Well," said the lawyer, exasperated, "get ready to spend between thirty and forty thousand dollars before this adoption gets finalized."

"What!" we both said a little louder than we intended.

"By the time you get the paternity tests, court costs, and documents filed, it will probably be up to a year before this will all happen."

The room seemed to spin as my heart started feeling a most unbearable pain. I could not breathe. I picked Bella up and walked out into the waiting room, almost as if in a trance. Thirty to forty *thousand* dollars! We still had that and more of Aiden's school loans left, which ate away a huge chunk of our monthly income. Not to mention our mortgage, two car payments, the food costs, and bills for a few credit cards. "This is not going to happen, is it, God?" I asked fearfully.

Aiden appeared a few moments later, looking extremely distressed. "Let's go," he said abruptly. We walked out of the lawyer's office. As I strapped Bella into the back seat of our car, my mind raced for ideas on how we could get ahold of that money. I had no expensive jewelry or anything valuable to sell. We knew there was no one we dared borrow the money from. And adding more debt did not seem a wise thing to do. Both of us knew logically in our heads what had to happen, but our hearts kept us from uttering the wretchedly distasteful words.

With my spirit as heavy as a boulder, we drove slowly back to the home where we had picked Bella up not twenty-four hours earlier. I hesitated several times before handing her back to the caretaker. The people at the house sadly stated they would manage to place her with a foster family—but I didn't want to listen to any plans I would not get to be a part of.

I had never suffered the death of a child, but I empathized with all my heart and soul in that most emotionally devastating and tragic drive home without my daughter. The finality of the situation hit as Aiden turned our car onto the expressway to head home. I had, in fact, bonded with that baby girl as I rocked and held her during the night. The sobs wracked my body unlike anything I could ever have imagined. I cried until I could not expel a single tear more.

I was depressed for several months. I wanted absolutely nothing to do with anything involving babies or adoption. The pain was still very fresh. I could feel only anger when asked if we were "having" any more children. I was still a new Christian at the time. I could not understand why God had allowed me to see and hold that baby if it was not going to be possible to raise her. I thought to myself, "Why wouldn't God want us to adopt this helpless baby? What's wrong with us? We must *not* be the kind of parents we should be—that's why!"

Of course I know better now. There is a reason that Satan is called the Deceiver. Unfortunately, approximately six months passed before I peeked out, though spiritually bruised and battered, and resumed normal activities at my sons' schools and the church. The boys were too young to really understand what was going on, so I just told them that their little sister was not able to come home. They never questioned why. I am thankful that they never brought it up again.

Chapter 5

Fresh Start

About a year later, our first cozy home, which had been on the market for more than a year and a half, had finally sold. Using profits from the sale, we paid off a tiny portion of Aiden's school debt. We decided to rent another home briefly while trying to figure out how we could afford to buy or build. We had just signed a new six-month lease on our rental home when we received news, late one night, of the passing of Aiden's father.

My husband and his father had been estranged on and off for a long time, but when his father had been diagnosed with cancer, they had reconciled. We were extremely surprised to discover later that Aiden's father had left a generous sum of money to be divided equally among his three children. We used some of the inheritance to pay off Aiden's school loans completely; we also had enough left over for a down payment to build a larger home, so we decided to use it for just that.

You're probably wondering why we didn't try looking for Bella. Unfortunately, fear had always played a big role in my decision making up until that point, and this was no exception. In my mind, I wanted to picture Bella with two very loving parents in a nice little home, growing up healthy and strong and well-loved. What I feared was the complete opposite. I feared she was abused or worse. Additionally, I knew I would not be able to live with myself if she were—I couldn't even bring myself to think the word—deceased. So, we opted for what probably does not make sense to most people. We opted to just not know. I imagined Bella as I thought she ought to be.

In 2005, we had been in the southern Texas region for over ten years, and Aiden was starting to outgrow his position at work. We discussed the situation. Within a few months, an employment agency called to inform him of an interested company east of Dallas, Texas. We were excited at the opportunity to live in a big city again, with all the advantages and opportunities that could arise for our boys and ourselves. The hardest part of it all would be leaving the house and nearby family members as well as close friends we had all grown to love. The job application process lasted a few months.

When we received word that Aiden had been hired, we once again put our home up for sale. For several months, we lived apart on weekdays as Aiden made a once-weekly commute to and from Dallas. We decided simply to lease our home rather than try to sell it right then. We found a home to rent in the Dallas area. Aiden, I, and our two boys moved there together.

While I did not try to locate Bella, I thought about her often. I wondered what she looked like and whether she was okay. Had she been adopted? Where was she living now? I knew I had to stop torturing myself—I had to let her go. This was also a process.

I was blessed to stay home for a time with my boys as Aiden worked. However, since the boys were a little older at this point, I started to feel that restlessness in my heart once again; I wanted to volunteer in some capacity around the city.

I kept seeing colorful banners over traffic intersections in Dallas that said "CASA (Court Appointed Special Advocate) ... become a child advocate." I wondered about what a child advocate does. It sounded intriguing, so after a few weeks of pondering, I called.

I discovered that a child advocate is a volunteer who spends time with a child in the foster care or temporary placement system. Child advocates assist the government's Child Protective Services, whose caseworkers are inundated with up to forty cases per worker at times. An advocate usually devotes more time than the caseworker is able to the children and the details of the case;

most advocates carry no more than two cases at a time. The advocate is also assigned to interview parents, teachers, counselors, or doctors. Then the advocate presents to the court a written and sometimes oral report. This provides the judge with plentiful information to decide what is best for the child.

The process to volunteer as a child advocate was going to evoke some less-than-desirable memories in my own past, I speculated. I sat through the classes and started learning the material, including statistics. I worried that I could not be subjective enough when it came time to interview a person alleged to have abused or neglected a child. How could I speak to someone if I had evidence that he or she was abusing a child?

In addition to what I was told in training, I learned recently that according to the *National Alliance to End Homelessness*, each year approximately 550,000 teens and young adults of age twenty-four or younger experience homelessness in the United States in a given year. This statistic floored me. How are so many children ending up without permanent homes?

Halfway through the training, the advocate candidates were required to watch fairly graphic video evidence from a court case where a man was abusing a nine-month-old infant. (We lost half the class after the video.) As I watched, my lungs started to tighten up. My heart rate sped up alarmingly; I felt like I was having an anxiety attack. I remembered having a similar feeling as a child.

Once the anxiety had lessened, I sat there feeling physically sick and spiritually exhausted. I thought, "How on earth can I possibly sit in the same room with an alleged child abuser—much less speak to and not want to strangle the person?"

No sooner had that question escaped my thoughts than I felt God's gentle nudging of my memory about a book I had recently read, called *The Shack*, by William P. Young. In that novel, a man's youngest daughter is kidnapped and murdered. After enduring an unfathomable time of sorrow and then anger, God's perspective on humankind's sinful nature is shown in a most creative and amazing way. The lesson is that though we love and mourn the loss of a child, God, in his great love, mourns the loss of the souls of all his spiritual children more than we could ever know or imagine. Please understand that I do not intend to discount anyone who has lived through the devastation of losing a child. I give this example only to demonstrate that I personally was not given the authority here on earth to judge another human being. That is God's right. I had to remind myself daily of this little fact.

After some prayer, I decided to continue. Eventually all the paperwork and background checks were completed, and I obtained my official badge as a CASA volunteer.

Being a newbie at CASA, I was allowed only one case at a time. By the end of my first assignment, which involved a little four-year-old girl, I knew where my heart was taking me once more.

Chapter 6

Doing It Right This Time?

We had finally sold our home! We had been leasing a fairly inexpensive home for two years, hoping ultimately to build a new home in the country. We moved into that new home on Christmas Eve 2007.

My husband and I revisited the idea of adopting. We decided that this time we would have all the information we could possibly get before meeting our daughter. We took the introductory courses at an adoption agency from February through April 2008.

We cleaned our home spotless for the initial visit and family interview. In regard to how we kept our home, we were not an obsessive-compulsive family by any means. We were not slobs either. However, as I suddenly noticed every dust bunny and every picture out of place, I was terrified we wouldn't pass muster. Ellen, the caseworker, toured our new home and asked *very* personal questions about each of us. I grew concerned again that we weren't the optimal adoptive family. I thought about all the times that Aiden and I had yelled at the boys or let them watch television for way more time than was recommended by pediatricians. I recalled whether I had served take-out meals to my family more than twice a week. Also, my husband and I had argued a little too loudly more times than I cared to remember. Adoptive parents were always smiling and never fought, right? I tried to conjure up an image of June Cleaver in my head. Would the pearls be too much with my blue jeans, I wondered? We were also firm believers in corporal punishment for continuous acts of disobedience or dangerous behavior. Had we spanked our boys or given them the "stink eye" one too many times when they misbehaved? Would they rat us out and say we were terrible parents during their own private interviews? The caseworker departed with not so much as a hint about whether we had passed the interview. We were left to wonder until we heard from her again.

Fortunately, perfection was not a prerequisite to adopt a child! The adoption agency asked us which gender, age, and race we were looking for. We both knew we wanted a girl. As to the age, we had been looking online at different adoption websites and there were countless children, mostly in the age range of two to sixteen, who were in need of a home. We opted for the age range of two to six, as we supposed that it would be somewhat easier to instill our own family's values and morals in a young child. As for the race, neither I nor Aiden set limits about the race of the child, but we prayed that she would be healthy.

Part of me did long for a child who looked somewhat like me, as Aiden had dominated the gene pool expression in our two biological sons. Ellen informed us that they had no cases with little girls of the targeted age at the moment. She estimated, however, that our daughter would arrive within a year. Aiden and I discussed it later that evening. We both agreed that since we had been in our home only four months, it was okay to wait awhile to see how our finances looked. We had recently incurred many expenses in furnishing the new house. Anyway, we said to each other, if God wants us to have a child right now, he will just drop her in our laps—famous last words.

In May 2008, about a month after we had passed our home inspection, I sat at work in the morning, calculating interest percentages. I had no inkling of how all our lives were about to change forever. I had found this part-time job in 2006 as an oil and gas accountant; I worked sixteen to twenty hours weekly. Thus, I was able to keep up with my CASA duties as well.

At work, I shared an office with the controller, to whom I reported. He was a sweet and very polite elderly gentleman who made my job easy to do. I had just celebrated my second anniversary at work. I was eagerly anticipating taking some vacation days.

At this time, Aiden and I were planning a vacation that we had previously postponed. About a year earlier, we had carefully planned a trip to the island of Nassau in the Bahamas. We had saved some of the money Aiden had received from his previous employer when he had left. The day before our plane was to depart, we received the devastating news of my dear Aunt Carrie's death. She had been battling and suffering with ovarian cancer for years. Mercifully for her, but painfully for us, she had been taken in the middle of the night. My heart was broken as I remembered the countless bicycle rides and talks, the many trips in her little blue Volkswagen Beetle to visit the ice cream shop. She was the ear who listened to me from the time I could speak to the time my boys were at the ages they could speak and more. My sweet boys and husband knew I could not take that vacation and enjoy any part of it. My heart would not be in it. I needed to be there for Aunt Carrie's funeral. Aiden canceled all the arrangements.

I had not been scheduled to speak at the funeral, as I had felt it would be impossible. As usual, God knew better. I ended up sharing an extremely personal account of a time when God had used nature itself to impress his love upon me when I had serious doubts of his existence. I would like to believe that perhaps this had an impact on the faith of many family members and friends that day. We sometimes struggle to see the good when we are mourning or going through some difficult times, but I knew I was meant to be there.

Because of timing for both Aiden and I at work, we were not able to reschedule our trip until the following year. So, as I sat there imagining the beautiful beaches and crystal clear water, my phone rang loudly, interrupting my daydream. Distractedly, I shuffled through my purse to answer it. I saw that the number looked somewhat familiar, but I could not place it immediately.

"Hi, Sophia!" said a cheery voice on the other end.

"Oh, hi, Ellen," I said, finally recognizing the lady who owned and headed the adoption agency. I assumed she had forgotten to get some other information, as we had recently passed the federal and state criminal background checks. "How are you?" I asked.

"Good," she said. "I have some news."

"Okay," I replied, intrigued, unsure of where she was going.

"Well," she said, "I have here in my office a little girl of five years. Her biological mom just signed the parental termination papers. And if you would like to adopt the girl, she's available."

I was speechless. The silence seemed unending. "What, what do you mean?" I asked, petrified. "We can't possibly be able to come get her just like that, can we?" I felt there had to be a catch somewhere. And besides, Aiden and I had just decided to wait awhile, hadn't we?

"Well," Ellen said, "I have five couples currently in the system. You guys are one of the two couples that have no race preference on your file. I tried calling the other couple as well and left a message, but you answered first. So I am giving you the option to come meet this girl and possibly place her in your home."

The room seemed to spin for a minute as I continued to ask Ellen question after question. I thought, "We're leaving in a week for the trip we rescheduled! We can't adopt a child right now! Oh no! The boys will *never* love her if we cancel our trip *again*!"

Worriedly, I asked Ellen, "You're positive her mother has relinquished her rights?"

"Positive!" said Ellen.

"What about her biological father?" I asked.

"He's deceased," she said somberly. "I'm waiting on a death certificate that should be here within the week. Also, the biological mom informed us that they have moved around for most of the child's life and that the child spent most of her time with relatives and friends. The mother claims she did not really spend much time with her."

It seemed that might make things easier. "What is the girl's name?" I asked.

"Her name is Estelle," replied Ellen.

"What nationality is she?"

"She is half African-American and half Hispanic," Ellen answered.

"What does she look like?" I was starting to get excited. I tried to picture the girl in my mind.

"She's kind of tall for her age," Ellen said. "Long, curly black hair. Medium-to dark-toned skin. Health records are up to date. She is quite intelligent, too, based upon our conversations this afternoon," Ellen said, bemused.

I did not know what to ask next. "Well," I said, a little unsure, "I'll have to call Aiden and talk to him." I also reminded Ellen that we were traveling out of the country the following week.

"Okay," she said, "but I will have to find a place for her to stay tonight. I will call one of the foster homes I have on file."

My mouth went dry as I considered this aspect. If this girl was really to be our daughter, would I want her to stay with strangers? "What if something happened to her?" bellowed my over-active imagination. "I'll get right back with you!" I said quickly. I hung up and dialed Aiden's work phone as fast as I could, as my mind went into hyper speed.

As usual, Aiden could not answer, as he had to attend countless work meetings every day. I left a detailed message and waited for what seemed like forever for him to respond. I could not concentrate on my percentage calculations that morning until Aiden finally called almost two hours later!

I recounted to him all the information I had been given. We discussed the trip but made no decisions on that. We talked for a good thirty minutes about why this could be happening now. We both remembered the statement we had made a month before: "If God wants us to have another child, he will just drop her in our lap." The dropping had been done. We agreed that we needed to go get her. As soon as we hung up, I phoned the agency and said we were on our way.

Chapter 7

But … She Doesn't Look Anything Like Me

As I hung up the phone and let my bosses know what had just occurred, I felt myself becoming emotional. I told myself, "I can't believe I'm meeting my daughter today. I can't wait to pick her up and hold her." My memory scooted itself back to Bella for a second, and my heart seemed to shrivel with the fear of the possibility of more pain. "No!" I thought, reminding myself of the differences. "*This* mother has relinquished her rights. The biological father is deceased, unfortunately for the child. This is *our* child this time!"

With congratulations coming from my coworkers, I headed out the door. Then I remembered that we did not have a single thing at home to give this child other than a spare bedroom. I jumped in my car and quickly dialed back to the agency to find out what the child had in her possession.

As I surmised, she had little—only a few articles of clothing, some books, and a picture or two. I ran to the nearest Target (yes, I have a knack for going there when I need a variety of things with lots of choices!). I remembered the clothing sizes Ellen had given me and felt surely she had been mistaken. I assumed the child would need smaller sizes. She was only five, after all.

I picked out some pajamas, shorts, and T-shirts. I perused the aisles and located a little girl's comforter, sheets, and a pretty pink blanket. I also bought her some little plates and cups. I raced home with my new purchases. I tried to turn the guest room into a somewhat stereotypical portrait of a little girl's room. I told myself that we could shop for more things later. We would have to find some way to afford it.

As I organized her room and waited for Aiden to arrive home, I wracked my brain, trying to figure out what to do about the trip. Maybe our new daughter could come with us? I figured we could try to somehow manage another ticket but … ooh the passport … how would that work? In the year before, we had gone through the rigorous passport application process for our boys, and it had taken a while for the passports to arrive. I had heard of an extra fee for expedited processing. I was wondering about it when my sons, Noah and Daniel, walked in from school.

"What are you doing, Mom?" asked Noah, the eldest.

"Good grief!" I thought. I had forgotten that the boys had no idea about our decision of that day! They had also gone through the preparations about what it would mean to have a non-biological sister and the situations that might come up. We had also read them some of the lessons the adoption agency had given us. "Sit down, guys," I said with a smile. "I have some exciting news."

They barely even blinked when I told them. "You're going today, now, to go get her?" asked Noah.

"Yup!" I said. "You guys ready to be big brothers?"

"I think so," they said almost simultaneously. They looked at each other, slightly bewildered, with goofy grins on their faces. Aiden burst through the door at that moment.

Aiden didn't even change out of his business suit; he and I hopped in the car and drove to the adoption agency. We sat in the parking lot a few minutes and prayed thankfully about this life-changing course we were about to embark on.

As regular attendees of a nondenominational church, we were more spiritual than religious. We believed then (and believe now) that if your heart is open to God and you follow the core biblical principles, God will guide you to make the right decisions through prayer. I was still in this place of certainty all the way to the agency's second floor office and as we knocked on the door and opened it.

We were greeted by Ellen and her assistant. They directed us toward another room to where "she" was. "Her name is Estelle," said Ellen.

While I still felt assurance that we were doing the right thing, I smiled nervously, my heart pounding with anticipation as we entered the room. And then I froze. I saw a girl sitting in the corner, enjoying a gummy snack. She looked directly at us and quickly rose to greet us.

Whatever certainty had remained suddenly hightailed out the door like a thoroughbred out of the gate at the Kentucky Derby. The young girl was much bigger than her age indicated. She looked more like eight years old than five. To me, she looked nothing at all like she had been described. I started to panic. I turned around and stared Aiden in the face. As fervently as I could, I mouthed, "I can't do this, I can't do this!"

The child came over to us and asked cautiously, "Are we going now? Are you the people that were coming to get me?"

"Uh, hold on, Sweetie," I said as calmly as I could. "We, uh, have to look over some paperwork." My emotions spun as I considered that I would *not* be able to carry her on my shoulders, *not* be able to rock her, *not* be able to wrap her sweetly in a towel and lift her up out of the tub while snuggling her on my lap. I turned to Aiden again. He looked at me with a peace I know he must have received from God himself. Aiden said calmly, "It's all going to be okay. We can do this."

I walked back to the front of the office. Trying to sound casual, I said to Ellen, "She's definitely bigger and taller than you said, huh? Are you positive she's five?"

"That's what her birth certificate states," Ellen said. "It appears to be genuine." She noticed my anxious face.

"Look," Ellen said, "I know this is all very sudden and you're both still in a bit of a shock at the speed at which this is happening. Maybe I should call the other couple back?" I turned around and closed my eyes briefly as I realized how this decision would tremendously alter all of our lives forever. Aiden was willing to proceed so, why was I feeling so conflicted?

I had walked into the adoption agency with the expectation of seeing a five-year-old girl's tiny, fragile face looking at me. I had envisioned that she would look like a mix of my husband and me. Instead, I was looking nervously at a girl with gorgeous cocoa skin—who seemed tall enough to be able to hold me in her lap. She picked up a huge, bulky, plastic container that held all her earthly possessions, looked me straight in the eye with a tear in hers, and bravely said, "Okay, I'm ready."

I could not believe my ears. I felt my eyes sting as I blinked back the tears. The courage it had taken for this five-year-old child to utter such words— after she had been informed that very morning that she would be put up for adoption—had melted my heart.

I looked at Ellen and said, "What do we need to sign?"

Chapter 8

This *Is* My Daughter

After we had filled out the remaining paperwork, Aiden carried the girl's plastic container to the trunk of our car.

We headed to the nearest grocery store to let her pick out some of her favorite fruit, snacks, shampoo, and bubble bath. As the three of us walked around the store together, I started noticing a few odd looks from people passing by. I could see them trying to figure out how the Caucasian man and the Hispanic woman had produced an African-American child. I brushed it off and just smiled.

We headed home and pulled into our driveway. Before the opening garage door had rolled to the top, the boys came bounding out. "Hey, guys, this is Estelle." I said excitedly. "She is going to be your new sister."

Without even skipping a beat, Noah said, "Come inside. You'll like it here."

Daniel smiled and said, "You wanna see your room?" I could not have been prouder of both my sons at that moment. Inside the house, I watched Estelle follow them from room to room. They gave her the grand tour of the house.

As night approached, I became concerned about how well she would sleep. I decided to let her have a bubble bath in our master bath, even though she had the use of her own bathroom. Our tub was a little bigger, and I wanted her to feel like she could be comfortable throughout the home.

"What kind of bedtime stories do you like?" I asked as we put on her pajamas. "I don't know," she said, a little confused.

"Well," I said, "do you like *Disney* stories or *Madeline* or *Little Bear*?" She continued to stare, blank faced, at me. After a minute, as I looked around unsurely, I decided to dig some of the boys' old books out of the attic. I read to her that night. She fell asleep fairly quickly.

Before I knew it, morning had come. I jumped out of my bed, realizing I had slept all through the night and had not heard a peep from Estelle's room. "Well, I'm not making the finals list for Mother of the Year!" I said to myself. I quickly walked to her bedroom to check on her. As I opened the door, she was already sitting up in bed; she looked at me.

"Is this a dream?" Estelle asked.

"Is what a dream, Honey?" I replied.

"Are you a dream? This house? My room?"

I didn't know how to tell her that she was not imagining all this. I became concerned that she really could not grasp the reality of all that had happened to her in the last twenty-four hours. How could she at five years old? I could barely believe it at the age of thirty-eight!

"Well," I replied, "no, this is not a dream. You are really here and this is your very own room." I waited anxiously for her response. Would she start crying, screaming, or throwing things at me?

"Oh, okay," she said calmly. "I'm hungry."

"Great!" I said, utterly relieved.

Chapter 9

What about the Trip?

"One mountain down and fifty to go," I said to Aiden on the first morning of Estelle's new life in our household. "What are we going to do about our trip?" It was a week away. We had asked the agency about expediting a passport. None of the adoption paperwork was finalized; we were told that the processing would take up to six months. We technically were not Estelle's legal parents yet, according to the state of Texas. The agency offered to get a passport under its name since the agency *was* the legal guardian. However, I had nightmares of attempting to board a plane in another country and being accused of kidnapping a child, especially since she looked nothing like us.

After agonizing a few days, we decided to do what most people our age would do when we were up a creek without a paddle—beg our parents to come and be child sitters for a week! My husband's mother and stepfather lived in town but had planned a trip at the same time we had. So my parents were the next logical choice; they agreed to watch Estelle.

Aiden and I then had the not-so-pleasant task of explaining the situation to our new five-year-old daughter. She cried a few tears. But after we explained that she would be meeting her new grandparents—and that grandparents treated granddaughters like princesses—she seemed somewhat contented. (Yes, we bribed!)

I also explained the whole passport situation in five-year-old terminology. I told Estelle, she did not yet have our last name and was not legally ours.

I had received a generous "baby shower" gift card from my coworkers. I used it to buy necessary items for Estelle *and,* of course, more importantly, "guilt" gifts.

My parents arrived the day before our departure. Even now, I am and will forever be grateful that they were generous enough to do this for us. When I was growing up, I did not have the relationship I desired with my parents, as I was raised as they were raised: children are to be seen and not heard.

I was so moved by the eagerness and cheerfulness in which my parents accepted the task of watching Estelle for an entire week that I forgave my parents all resentment and hurt I had harbored into adulthood. From the start, they loved and accepted Estelle as if she were their own flesh and blood.

We left on our trip, still feeling a little guilty and having heavy hearts that we could not take Estelle with us. Our first purchase after arriving on the island was a phone card; we used it to call her every evening before she went to bed. She sounded happy and content. Grandma and Grandpa had taken her on outings and shopping trips. While we still felt a little down, we eventually realized that the trip would have been quite overwhelming and stressful for Estelle at that age.

Estelle was the first granddaughter in our family (my sister and I had each borne two sons). Aiden and I so wanted Estelle to feel special about her exclusive status. We reiterated it to her frequently when we conversed on the phone.

Five days flew by quickly, and before we knew it, Estelle and my parents were picking us up at the airport. "Hi, Mom!" she said. She gave me a big hug.

I was taken aback. I hugged her in return, saying, "Hi, Sweetie, how are you?"

"Great!" she replied happily. "Grandma and Grandpa let me have candy and ice cream every day!"

"Oh boy," I said to Aiden. "It's going to be fun when we tell her that little ritual is *not* going to be permanent."

Chapter 10

Do I Want to Meet *Her*?

We had been back from our trip about a week and a half when I got a call from the adoption agency. The news was that Estelle's biological mother, Tina, was requesting to meet us. We had mutually agreed, when signing all the legal paperwork, that this was to be a *semi-closed* adoption. It meant that contact between the biological mother and Estelle would be made by written letters only. In comparison, it is called an *open* adoption when the biological parents have visits and open communication with the child. In a *closed* adoption, there is absolutely no contact. I struggled with meeting the biological mother, because I feared that she may want Estelle back and there was some legal loophole that had been overlooked.

After some discussion about the pros and cons of meeting Estelle's birth mother, we decided to go. I knew that if I had been in her situation, I would want to—at the very least—meet the people who would be raising my child. I desired that the woman see we were not ax murderer psychopaths.

On the way to the meeting, I started thinking, "What kind of mother could tell her child in the morning that she was being put up for adoption and then immediately take her to an agency that very same day? Why would she let the child become so unhealthy?" My mamma-bear instinct and judgmental alter ego started to rear their ugly heads.

We could not tell Estelle where we were going, because we knew that it would be too much for her. She had also mentioned recently that she was really missing her little sister. We had found out later her younger sister had been placed for adoption two weeks earlier with a couple from out of state.

I carried a letter that I had helped Estelle write to her biological mother. We referred to her by her proper name, Tina, since we had been instructed to encourage Estelle to stop calling the woman Mommy.

We also brought some pictures we had recently taken of Estelle.

I walked into the building ready to give this woman a talking to. But as we entered the room, I looked into the tear-stained face with the pained eyes resembling my daughter's. I saw the look of complete hopelessness. And my anger gave way to compassion. Tina had brought what few baby pictures she had left of Estelle. That's when we found out Estelle had not one but *two* younger half-sisters! The youngest still lived with her biological father.

Tina asked how Estelle was coping. I told Tina of all the activities that Estelle had been keeping herself busy with and how bright and polite she was.

When Tina described the morning of the adoption, Aiden and I started to realize just how much like an adult our little five-year-old was. Tina said that before taking Estelle to school, Tina had told Estelle that she was going to be put up for adoption. Estelle had replied patiently, "Uh, we'll talk about that when we get home, okay?"

Tina explained that she had been homeless for a while and had been struggling to hold on to a job. She had been moving from house to house, living with family members and friends. While she wanted stability and a good home life for her children, she knew that she could not provide it at that time.

It finally hit me that this mother had made a lot of bad choices but was not a bad person. By placing Estelle for adoption, this mother had decided upon what she knew in her heart to be the best solution. How could I dislike a mother who chose to give birth to her child, to give life? How could I judge a mother who made one of the hardest decisions she could ever make, by admitting that she herself was not the best choice to raise her children but that someone else could do a better job? My heart broke for her predicament.

31

We sobbed in each other's arms when we said goodbye. Tina asked me to please take good care of her baby. I promised that I would.

I had learned many lessons in life and thought I had figured out quite a few things. On that day, I realized I had not even scratched the surface.

Shortly after our meeting, I was able to take about a week off from work to spend some time with Estelle and get to know her better. We went on a few shopping trips so she could pick out some room décor and more articles of clothing. Finding a movie to watch was a little tough, as I wanted to be sure not to take her to anything that might remind her of her biological mother. Also, I had not realized how many movies make the stepmother or the adoptive parent out to be the bad guy (one encouraging exception was *Stuart Little*). I was annoyed and dismayed at such negative portrayals of non-biological parents.

Our next challenge was child care for our girl, who was not yet six years old. Our oldest son, Noah, was only thirteen at the time; we would let him watch his younger brother and Estelle at home alone for only one or two hours at a stretch. I was working part time and still volunteering at CASA during the summer of 2008. Fortunately, Aiden's mom lived across town; we were grateful that she watched Estelle a few hours each day through the middle of July. As it was quite a drive for us to get to my mother-in-law's home, however, we opted to put Estelle in a local church day camp for the rest of the summer.

Chapter 11

Constant road hazzards

One day at the beginning of July, Ellen called and informed us that all the paperwork had been processed! The adoption would be finalized in court at the next available session two weeks later.

"Two weeks?" I asked, quite shocked. "You said it would be at least six to eight months. How is this possible?"

"I can't believe it!" said Ellen. "I've yet to have a case go so quickly. Isn't that crazy?"

I had known, when we had first met Estelle, that it was the right decision to bring her home with us. But as time went on and challenging situations arose, I found myself doubting our decision. I wondered why I wasn't having the warm fuzzy feelings I thought I should have been experiencing by then. Why was it so hard to get close to this child? I started to think that maybe we weren't the best choice for her.

As the weeks progressed and Estelle and I spent more time together, I started to wince at some of the comments she made. When we took her ice skating one afternoon, she asked me what the rink's address was. I asked her why she needed the address, since I would be taking her if she returned.

She replied, "Oh, I need to know so Tina and I can go later."

"Oh, all right," I said, a little confused.

On another outing, I took us both for pedicures. After we had left the shop, Estelle asked me it's name. When I told her, she happily said, "Oh, Tina will love that place; we'll do that together."

Estelle would also tell me Tina's favorite foods, colors, movies, and places. I thought to myself, "This child knows a lot about a mother she supposedly never spent much time with." I started to get concerned.

I mentioned my distress to Aiden. We decided to call the agency to ask for help. They had been keeping track of our progress. After adopting, we had been required to attend two counseling sessions for Estelle's and our family's well-being. According to the counselor, all had seemed well. She had assured me we were doing everything possible for Estelle.

Around this time, I had met a woman at our church who had adopted internationally and domestically through a foster care agency. I figured if anyone would know whether our situation was normal, she would. After a few conversations, she assured us this was perfectly normal, just as the agency had. "Children like to make up a fantasy in their heads," they said. "It is just a coping mechanism."

"But, she seems to know so much detail about her bio-mom!" I replied. I started to get the feeling that something was not right. I felt in my gut that we had not received the whole story.

A few months passed, and things seemed to be progressing for the better. School was a welcome relief; I had started to feel ill at ease from our little outings. It had seemed that every time we were alone together, Estelle would share some new story about a fun-loving occasion she had experienced with Tina.

Some stories, I would find out later, were *not* so fun loving. I began to notice Estelle's reactions of anxiety and discomfort regarding police; it wasn't until a few months later that I understood why. We found out that Estelle had been taught to fear police and had actually been asked to lie to them on different occasions. I knew it would not be easy to get her to change her point of view in this situation, but I knew we had to try. I also had to be cautious whenever I attempted to brush a strand of hair off her face or reach for her. Her immediate reaction was to jerk away as if I were going to harm her. I had not been naive enough to think she was going to come to us problem free, especially with my experience with my CASA cases, but I had thought that after reading Estelle's case file, we had gotten most of the information.

A year or so had passed fairly uneventfully after the official adoption, and another summer had almost come to an end. I had left my fourteen-year-old son to sit for an hour one morning in July as I ran to the grocery store for a few items. I had returned, and the boys were helping to bring the bags into the house, when I heard crying coming from Estelle's room. I walked in to find her holding one of the pictures she had been given by Tina the day Estelle had been taken to the agency.

Estelle had taken the picture out of the foam picture frame it had been encased in. She turned it over and sobbed. "Can I please call my mom! Please let me, please!" I saw what she was looking at, and I just gasped. Tina had put a telephone number on the back of the picture. "She told me to call her if I needed to!" Estelle continued to sob. My fear turned to anger. I could not believe what I was seeing and hearing! "She said I would just be here a little while; then she would come get me!" Estelle cried out.

I took the picture from her. I was terrified that perhaps she had tried to call Tina already. My fear had come from the stories Estelle had been telling me of seeing physical fights between her bio-mom and family. I also was concerned about why Estelle had been asked to lie to police when she was living with Tina. Estelle had also mentioned witnessing things of an adult nature when the adults in question assumed she was sleeping. "What did Tina say to you about us adopting you, Estelle?" I asked sternly.

After about a twenty-minute conversation, I ascertained what it all had boiled down to for Estelle: Tina advised her to get all she could get from us and in time, Tina would be back for Estelle! "This can't be happening, this can't be happening!" I bellowed in my mind. I was nearly hysterical as I got in my car and left the house. I had to get away from there and think. Everything that Estelle had said over the last year and a half had finally made sense. I called the agency and irately told them of the day's events and asked if they knew of Tina's whereabouts.

"She doesn't have a permanent address," Ellen said, "but we have a phone number and we'll get to the bottom of it." I waited for what seemed like hours before I got a call back.

"Well, I can assure you, after speaking to Tina, she has no intention of coming back to get Estelle," Ellen stated, as if it were a matter of fact.

"How can you be so sure?" I asked, highly distressed.

"She understood the terms," Ellen said plainly. "She knows that her children are better off. She does realize her life and choices were not the best thing for them." I listened silently as Ellen concluded. "Tina said she told Estelle those things to make herself feel less guilty about placing Estelle."

The explanations did nothing to calm me. "But now how am I going to be able to explain this to a seven-year-old?" I asked irately.

"Well … I think another trip to the counselor is probably in order," replied Ellen.

When I hung up, I was still completely furious. My mind raced as I thought to myself, "Here I am, pouring my life, my heart and soul into someone else's child. Then as soon as she turns eighteen, she's just going to turn around and leave me to go find her 'real mother'! She's going to become who knows what and completely break my heart!"

I continued to be distressed and angry when once again I felt God's prompting of my spirit. "Sophia," he seemed to whisper, "What makes you think your biological children can't do that to you? When are you going to realize that you don't have control over *any* of them?"

I cried as the realization about the truth of the matter sunk in. These lessons on control were especially difficult for people who have been abused as children, as I had been. I had always struggled in particular with this issue that stealthily crept in and out of my life.

Aiden and I sat down with Estelle that night and had a long discussion about what it meant to be adopted. Soon afterward, the three of us discussed it further with a counselor in a counseling session. The session went a little better than we had anticipated. Life seemed to move on—but not always as expected.

Birthdays and Mother's Days seemed to always be times for Estelle to act up a bit or start to revert to certain toddler-like behavior. I assumed it was her way of coping with the stress and constant reminder that this was a permanent, not temporary, situation. Aiden and I struggled with the emotional and sometimes financial stress of the situations we found ourselves encountering each week or month.

Another issue for which I thought I had prepared myself was Estelle's eating style and habits. I had learned through the adoption preparation and the CASA classes that many foster and adopted children use food to self soothe. They might hoard food in a place they think will be as inconspicuous as possible, in order to assure themselves a meal. Of course, I made sure all the kids had three meals a day plus plenty of healthy snacks from which to choose. However, somewhat to our surprise, Estelle would hoard food.

Of course, Halloween and Christmas made it quite difficult to keep up with every snack the kids were indulging in. Following the first Halloween together with Estelle, we thought it best that she could have a few snack-size candies at a time. The rest would remain in a jar on the highest shelf in the pantry. We planned to dole out the candies one at a time on certain occasions, not daily and certainly not throughout the day. I discovered that the candies were disappearing from the container faster than I was handing them out. I confronted all three children one afternoon after I returned from work. The boys were adamant that they had not been in the jar. Estelle was even more adamant that she would not dare and could not reach it anyway. She furthermore said I was free to search her room and the boys' rooms to test her honesty.

After finding no evidence in her room, I quickly went upstairs to our younger son Daniel's room. There in the middle of the floor, in plain sight for me to see, were three candy wrappers randomly strewn about. I could not believe the boys had lied to me; thus far in their young lives, they had been very good about telling the truth. I scolded them while they stared at me blank faced. They remained adamant that neither one had eaten the candy.

I was upset with their dishonesty and was reading in my room later that evening when a soft knock on the door caused me to look up. "Come in," I said.

It was Estelle, appearing highly distressed and uncomfortable. "Hi, Mom. Can I talk to you?" she said.

"Sure," I said. "What's up?

"Well," she said, "I'm scared to tell you something, because I know you're gonna be mad."

"What is it?" I asked tentatively.

"I, um … it was me who put the wrappers in Daniel's room. I wanted you to think he ate the candies."

My first thought was "How ingenious!" But I had to keep my composure and look as stern as possible. "Why would you do that?" I asked.

"Because I wanted the candy," she said, starting to tear up.

"What made you come and tell me?" I asked hopefully.

She cried out, "Because you said if I told the truth, you wouldn't be as mad."

I had mixed emotions as she said this to me. We had caught her lying about what she had been eating, but this was the first time she had admitted it. I felt that we were finally making some progress. Needless to say, I let her go **mostly** unpunished for her minor transgression (by the end of the week, our home's baseboards were much cleaner). She apologized to her brothers as well. They did not let her forget about it for quite a while. She still has her sugar fixes occasionally but comes clean with them—most of the time.

Chapter 12

Why Does Dad Have to Pick Me Up from School?

Our lives continued to be fast paced. I worked part time and cooked four to five times per week. I was involved with several projects. Additionally, I took care of the grocery shopping, kids' appointments, laundry, and all the other little things most mothers attend to in a given week. Because of this, time seemed to be going at warp speed. Aiden worked an hour from our home, so, unfortunately, most of these tedious tasks fell on me. However, his work pace had slowed down a bit for a spell and he had been leaving work right at 5:00 p.m., which was a miracle in itself. I was thrilled at the prospect of having some extra help for a while.

We paid for after-school care so Estelle could play with her school friends and enjoy organized activities. I had asked Aiden to pick her up on the way home a few times. On one particular evening, I noticed Estelle looking a little upset. "All right, what's wrong?" I asked as I was saying good night.

She started to speak and then stopped herself. She was quiet for a while before speaking again. "I don't want Dad picking me up from school anymore," she said with an annoyed tone.

"Why?" I replied. "What's the problem?" I wondered whether he had called her his "little baby" in front of her friends. Or had he made a goofy joke?

"People have been asking me why my dad is white," she said, teary eyed. "They're starting to ask if I'm adopted. If my parents were both dark skinned like me, no one would know or even ask if I was adopted! I don't want anyone to know!"

I closed my eyes. Before I drew my next breath, I knew, by God's grace, exactly what she needed to hear. "But what about me?" I said. "I'm also lighter than you are."

"I had a couple of people mention it," she said somberly, "but more people noticed when Dad came in."

"Estelle," I said as gently as I could, "your dad loves you very much. He doesn't care what color you are."

"I know!" she said. "But these kids keep asking me why I was adopted!"

"Oh great!" I thought, frustrated. Only eight years old and already she was having to respond to questions about that.

"Well," I said, "as to *why* you were adopted, you can say because we loved you—but only if you wish to give them an answer. As to our differences, your brothers have green eyes and light skin and I have brown eyes and am darker skinned than they are, especially in the winter when your brothers lose their tan. They don't look anything like me, either," I said, smiling. "Many people stared at me as I carried the boys around when they were little and they called me Mom. People always asked me if your brothers were mine, and I have to admit, it did bother me a bit."

Estelle smiled and said, "Oh, yeah, I didn't think about that."

"Also," I said, "don't you think God planned for our family to look like it does for a reason?"

"Why?" she asked curiously.

"Well," I replied, "when people see us walk into a restaurant or store together, their minds start trying to figure out who goes with whom and it inspires thoughts and questions in their minds. They start to wonder if we are a biological or blended family or maybe, just maybe, someone is adopted possibly."

"Yeah, I guess so," she stated, still needing convincing.

"Well," I said, "I don't have Bible verses memorized word for word like I probably should, but I know one of the verses that God is very adamant about is caring for widows and orphans." After I explained the definition of each and explained that *all* of us were actually adopted by God, which is what God desires for all orphans, her smile grew even wider.

"Mom," she said, "I want Dad to pick me up after school every day!"

Chapter 13

A Storm Is Brewing

I could not believe we were a month and a half from the end of the school year! Estelle's third anniversary of joining our family was approaching. She was charging through the fourth grade with flying colors. We began bragging to extended family and friends that Estelle was "a social butterfly and a teacher's pet in most of her classes." It had been a pretty good school year for Estelle. She excelled at her studies and brought home mostly A's on her report card and conduct card.

Thus, I started to get concerned as I received multiple notices from her teacher that week. First, Estelle had stolen a pencil from a classmate. The next day it was a sticker from the teacher. The following day Estelle had lied to the teacher and been caught. I went in for a conference with her teacher. We concluded that it had all resulted from the latest correspondence Estelle had received from her bio-mom, the week before.

Since we had agreed on the semi-closed adoption, Tina had been writing two to three times a year. I helped Estelle write responses. She was usually very stressed during these times and could never think of anything to say. I noticed that her behavior would change for about a week and then she would return to her usual cheery self. By this time, Estelle was nine years old. She was capable, by herself, of reading all the letters from her bio-mom and replying to them. Estelle still chose for me to read the letters with her and to help prepare replies. We had reduced the counseling sessions to only one or two a year. Our original counselor had retired, so we had switched to a different counselor.

I was a little nervous whenever that envelope from the agency arrived in the mail. It meant that Estelle would be reminded of her bio-mom, generating a wave of emotions and, worst of all, fresh agonizing pain. I tried earnestly to make it a positive time and a reminder to her that she was not forgotten but loved. I also felt guilty on occasion because I did not feel as close to Estelle as I thought I would feel by that time. I think we both put a little wall between us for fear of being hurt again.

It had been about a week since Tina's latest letter, and I noticed Estelle back talking and becoming a little aggressive. She was also becoming uncharacteristically disrespectful. After a long, drawn-out confrontation, she finally let spill what had been apparently plaguing her for years. She told us we must have forced her bio-mom to sell her to us and we must have given her bio-mom a lot of money. I was taken aback, shocked, and just heartbroken about all the pain and conflicting emotions that would lead Estelle to such a conclusion in her mind.

Once again, my go-to was the adoption agency; I called to seek advice on what to do. Since it had been almost three years since the adoption, they suggested a visit to the office. The agency could confirm to Estelle directly that everything was truly legal and that we had not bought her from her biological mother. The agency also suggested that Estelle go to an individual counseling appointment immediately after our visit. As we headed to the agency, I felt as if I would soon be sick to my stomach. I knew the insurmountable agony that was about to befall my sweet daughter.

With Aiden and I present, Ellen recounted to Estelle the events of the day we came to pick her up. Estelle started to look angry. She then just sobbed quietly and gazed out the window. I wished with all my heart that I could take the pain away. We headed to the counselor's office as soon as we were done at the agency. Estelle entered the counselor's office; Aiden and I waited outside for an agonizing hour. When Estelle returned, she looked unfazed and nonchalant. I looked quickly at the counselor and gestured with my eyes for a quick conference of our own.

"Should we schedule next week or later on this week?" I asked anxiously.

"No, I think she's doing okay," said the counselor confidently.

"Are you sure—maybe a couple weeks?" I asked again.

"Well, if you notice any acting out or you're having issues, sure, bring her back," she replied. I knew my daughter was strong, but this seemed to be too much to just go away on its own. I wanted to be hopeful; I figured the professionals knew what they were doing.

That week continued without occurrence at our home and the school. I thought maybe, just maybe, Estelle had somehow come to terms with all the latest events miraculously. I now know this was unrealistic, but occasionally I am overly optimistic and a tad naive.

The following week, I was heading to pick up my younger son, Daniel, at the middle school, which, unfortunately for us, is some distance away. I heard my phone ringing; I did not want to look away from the road but glanced at the phone momentarily. Recognizing the number for Estelle's school, I answered the call immediately.

"Hello, this is Mrs. Peterson, Estelle's teacher. How are you?" Her voice had a stern tone.

"Uh, I'm fine," I replied cautiously.

"Well," Mrs. Peterson said, "I have Estelle here and she and I have been discussing her lying to me this afternoon."

"Oh, no!" I said.

After a few minutes, Mrs. Peterson and I came to the conclusion that an immediate parent-teacher conference would be in order. I hung up. Within a few minutes I had arrived at Daniel's school and picked him up.

As we began the jaunt back toward the elementary school, which was less than a mile from our home, my phone rang again. I noticed the same number. I answered the phone, figuring Mrs. Peterson had forgotten to mention something. Her tone had changed dramatically from somewhat stern to completely excited.

"Mrs. Blake," she said, "I don't want you to panic, but your daughter is missing!"

"I'm sorry—what?" I said, panicking.

"Estelle—we can't find her anywhere," Mrs. Peterson said. "I sent her back to the after-school care center in the school and she somehow sneaked past them!"

"Please, God, help us!" I thought.

It had been exactly a week after the trip to the adoption agency.

"I knew it, I knew it," I said aloud. "I should have taken her back to the counselor, I should never have taken her to the agency—"

"Mrs. Blake!" the teacher said urgently. "Can you come to the school please? We have just notified the police department."

"I'm coming!" I yelled as I pressed down on the gas and started speeding toward the school.

The tears began to flow as every horrible scenario I could possibly think of started to play out in my mind. A highway stretched between our home and the school; I tried earnestly not to think of all the deer, rabbits and other animals that were regular victims of the cars hurtling by at sixty miles per hour. Semi-trucks constantly used that road as well. I simply began to pray. I considered what could happen if a stranger saw her walking and picked her up. I started to get frantic.

I called Aiden at work; within a matter of minutes he was in the car for the long drive home. I was about two miles from the school when a new number popped up on my phone. I answered the call.

"Mrs. Blake, I don't know if you remember me," said a familiar voice.

"Mrs. Gunther?" I said. Mrs. Gunther was a teacher from Estelle's school. She had taught Estelle in the first and second grade and had formed quite a bond with her.

"Yes," the teacher replied, her voice tense with emotion. "We still haven't found Estelle, but we got her friend Cassie to talk to the police when they interviewed her and her mother."

"Where is Estelle?" I asked, frightened.

"Cassie told us Estelle was planning to run away to find her biological mom," said Mrs. Gunther.

"Did she say how on earth she would try to do that?" I asked emphatically, trying desperately not to get even more hysterical.

"Estelle was supposed to go to Allie's house and look for her on Facebook, according to Allie."

"So, have the police gone there yet?" I asked, terrified.

"They're on the way there now," said Mrs. Gunther.

When I arrived at the front entrance of our subdivision, I noticed two police cars at the park that was located nearby. I promptly stopped and got out to speak with them. They had uncovered no trace of Estelle but had been interrogating walkers and joggers about whether they had seen a girl matching her description.

Because of her height and build, Estelle looked two to three years older than her true age, so most casual observers may have thought nothing of an apparent teenager walking through the neighborhood alone. The police questioned me. As I gave them our contact information, a call on the police officer's phone startled me, as if it had been a gun going off.

Estelle had been spotted walking in the back area of our neighborhood. We all jumped in our cars and took off toward that location. My mouth was dry and my stomach felt as if every intestine had decided to braid itself inside out.

I circled the neighborhood several times until I met up with one of the officers. He asked, "Have you gone back and checked to see if maybe she just decided to go home?"

"*No!*" I thought, as I shook my head. "Why didn't I check the house!"

"We'll go to your house if there is no sign of her elsewhere. We will ask you some more questions shortly," he said.

Reaching our home, I raced up the driveway and stopped the car. I flew into the house shouting her name. There was no response. I couldn't breathe. It felt like I would have an anxiety attack if not a stroke at any moment. It had been almost two hours since the first call had come from the school. I knew how intelligent Estelle was. "She could be anywhere by now," I thought in agony. I cried and prayed.

Aiden had finally made it home. I was updating him when a call came in on my phone once again. The chief of police had just received word from the school that a parent had called and said Estelle was at their home. It was in an area that was the farthest away, on one of the last streets in the back of the subdivision about two miles from the school. "Thank God! Thank God!" I said. My legs felt like they would collapse any second. My emotions ranged from relief to anger and then settled on empathy as I put myself in Estelle's position.

I knew that as she aged and matured, she would get a better grasp of her past history and a greater capacity to deal with events in her life as they happened. I realized that this sweet, intelligent child had never been given a real choice in her life-changing adoption or any major decision in her life. As I thought forward to the evening, when Aiden and I would gather up the words we wanted to speak into her life, I knew what we needed to do.

When we arrived at the other family's home, the chief of police approached us immediately. In a compassionate manner, she said, "It might be best if you let us bring your daughter to you. I have dealt with similar occurrences. It helps the child to understand the seriousness of the situation." She went on to say Estelle was very distraught that her attempt had been foiled. We took that into consideration. We decided to let them bring Estelle to our home. Aiden and I prayed during this time and discussed what we should do.

After what seemed like hours but was actually only about thirty minutes, our doorbell rang and our daughter appeared at the door. We called her into the family room and sat next to her. As I started to speak, she began to sob. "You're not going to want me anymore, are you!" she cried out.

"Yes, we do still want you," I said softly. "But I want you to *want* to stay. We love you and we want you here with us forever." She was looking at me. "It doesn't matter what you do," I said. "You can steal, lie, and do what you did today, but we will still love you and want you here with us."

Estelle tried with every fiber of her being to control her weeping. But she had internalized so many of her emotions for so long that they escaped like a tidal wave crashing upon a shore. I allowed her to calm herself before Aiden and I continued with a choice we felt might empower Estelle, as so many life changing decisions had been made without any consultation on her part. As adults, we realize a child is not capable of realizing the enormity of a decision, but as we put ourselves in her shoes, we started to understand how even feeling remotely like she had some say in her life, might give her some peace of mind.

"We have a thought," I stated, looking directly into her eyes. "Again, we don't want you to go, and you do mean the world to us. But, if you would like to just get through the next nine to ten years with a foster family, it will be hard for us to let you go, but we will let you do that if it is what you really want." Her eyes widened. "When you are eighteen years old, we will also help you find Tina if you would like." I let that sink in. "Or," I said, "You could stay here and continue your life here with us as our daughter. So, we want you to think it over tonight and don't give us an answer until the morning."

We knew that we did not want to let her go but wanted *her* to make that choice and not feel as if we were forcing her to stay. We prayed with her. Then we kissed her goodnight and put her to bed, as we awaited her big decision the next morning. After living with our daughter for years, and understanding more and more of who she was and how she processed problems, we felt this was the best decision we could make at this time.

The sun rose bright and early that morning as Aiden and I were preparing breakfast. In trotted Estelle with a big smile on her face. Aiden and I tried to act normally, without expressing anticipation. I poured Estelle a glass of juice. She sat down and blurted out, "Okay, I think I'll stay!" She grinned.

"We are so glad!" We both replied completely relieved.

A couple of weeks later, I contacted the adoption agency to find out, for Estelle's sake, whether they knew anything new about Tina's whereabouts and future plans. I had started to second guess myself again on our decision to permit only written contact between Estelle and Tina. Out of curiosity, I checked Facebook, but I did not see Tina listed.

About a month after that, I received a call from Ellen at the agency. She had recently spoken to Tina about Estelle's struggles and how confused Estelle was about Tina's explanations of what to expect from the adoption. Tina said it had been difficult to continue writing to Estelle, as it evoked painful memories and grief every time Tina put pen to paper. Ellen told Tina that while she was free to continue writing as often as she wanted, Ellen would send Estelle the correspondence only twice a year.

We have not heard from Tina again, and her whereabouts are unknown to us.

Estelle has released the idea of finding Tina for now, but I know we will cross that path again as we near Estelle's eighteenth birthday. I know we will get through that and any other uncontrollable life events with the help and grace of God. He has yet to let us down.

Chapter 14

You'll be in My Heart

It has been almost four years since that terrible day in April when we did not know where Estelle was. As I sit here writing this account of our adoption experiences, I am feeling very blessed. Life did not miraculously perfect itself since that April day. And we did not magically start doing everything right with any of our children.

We may not ever know the reasons why devastating and life-altering things happen to some of us. I believe, however, that we all make choices in our lives that map our future courses toward destinies that God wants for us. Choices that seem to be *mistakes* are opportunities for God to do his best work. There is a saying I have heard often and absolutely love. It states, "What Satan has meant to be destructive or bad God will turn around and use for good."

I know that is the case with my childhood abuse, as I believe it actually helped motivate me to become a children's advocate and ultimately adopting my daughter. This is my opinion of my own life, not a reference for anyone else who may have had a perfectly happy childhood. I know that on the day my five-year-old daughter heard she was being put up for adoption, the rug was yanked out from under her entire life. Yet, I've seen the tremendously positive impact Estelle has had on so many people we know and even people we've just met.

I adamantly believe that there is a particular reason our family is so diverse. It makes others notice us and ask questions, by which they find out we are an adoptive family. I know there are many of you out there who really want to ask families about adoption and are afraid of offending someone. My heart lights up when I see or hear of someone who is adopted or who has adopted a child. My heart breaks when I speak to others who aged out of foster care and, to this day, do not have a family to call their own.

People have asked us how we could love an adopted child like we love our biological children. The answer, I believe, is really quite simple. You already love each biological child in a different way, but you still love each one. It is the same for an adopted child. You want to discipline each child the same, but you can't always do that. In our experience, you have to discipline them differently, according to their personalities. As you certainly have read and heard, adopting is not always easy, but for us, it has been possible with God. Some children will have more needs; some will have less. And I can *guarantee* that neither you nor they will be perfect.

I pray wholeheartedly that as you read these honest and real-life accounts of our journey to adopt an older child, you won't be fearful or intimidated but instead will be truly inspired and motivated. If you adopt, you will have good and bad days. The bottom line is that a child who had virtually no hope of a promising future or life is receiving *hope*.

We have had trials, and there will be many more trials ahead, but I know that after all we have endured together, I would risk death for my daughter. I love Estelle more than anything and could not imagine my life without her. Though our faces may never mirror each other's faces, I pray that our hearts will forever mirror each other's hearts. I thank God for bringing her to us.

Each of my children has his or her own *Disney* theme song that I can't even get through without bawling like a baby. Noah's song is the *Toy Story 3* song "Moving On." Daniel's song is *Hercules*' "Go the Distance." And Estelle's song is "You'll Be in My Heart," which is Phil Collins' brilliantly written song in the movie *Tarzan*. Because the character *Tarzan* was loved unconditionally by his adoptive mother, the lyrics, *I know we're different but deep inside, we're not that different at all*, perfectly emulate the heart and intentions of so many foster and adoptive parents everywhere.

One particular line of the song always takes me back to that fateful day I met my courageous daughter Estelle for the first time. It will forever resound within me. *"For one so small, you seem so strong ..."* She most definitely *is*!

Printed in the United States
By Bookmasters